The Mayflower Compact

DAVID & PATRICIA ARMENTROUT

Rourke
Publishing LLC
Vero Beach, Florida 32964

DOCUMENTS THAT SHAPED THE NATION

www.rourkepublishing.com

PHOTO CREDITS: Cover Scene, Pages 12, 16, 23, 27, 29, 36, 38, 40 © North Wind Picture Archives. Title Page, Pages 4, 15 © James P. Rowan. Pages 6, 35 Artville, LLC. Page 7 from the Architect of the Capitol. Pages 10, 21 © Getty Images. Pages 25, 32, 43 © PhotoDisc, Inc. Cover Document and Pages 9, 17, 19, 30, 42, 43 from the Library of Congress

Title page: *Plymouth Rock is a 10-ton piece of granite that is the legendary landing spot of the Pilgrims.*

Editor: Frank Sloan

Cover and page design by Nicola Stratford

Library of Congress Cataloging-in-Publication Data

Armentrout, David, 1962-
 The Mayflower Compact / David and Patricia Armentrout.
   p. cm. -- (Documents that shaped the nation)
 Includes bibliographical references (p.   ) and index.
 ISBN 1-59515-229-6
 1. Mayflower (Ship)--Juvenile literature. 2. Mayflower Compact
(1620)--Juvenile literature. 3. Pilgrims (New Plymouth Colony)--Juvenile
literature. 4. Massachusetts--History--New Plymouth, 1620-1691--Juvenile
literature. I. Armentrout, Patricia, 1960- II. Title. III. Series:
Armentrout, David, 1962- Documents that shaped the nation.
 F68.A73 2004
 974.4'8202--dc22
                        2004014413

3365186

Printed in the USA

w/w

TABLE OF CONTENTS

THE PILGRIMS

Almost 400 years ago a group of people sailed across the Atlantic seeking religious freedom and a better life for themselves. We know them as **Pilgrims**. They called themselves Saints and Strangers.

After 66 days at sea, the Pilgrims arrived in safe harbor aboard their ship, the *Mayflower*. They did not leave the ship until they came to an agreement. The Pilgrims

wanted, in writing, a statement saying that they would support each other and work together for the good of the colony. They wanted to form their own government and choose their own leaders. This meant they would govern themselves. It was a type of leadership that they had never experienced before.

Plimoth Plantation is a museum that recreates the settlement built by the Pilgrims.

"Plimoth" is the old-fashioned spelling used by Governor William Bradford in his history of the colony. The museum adopted this spelling to differentiate the museum from the town of Plymouth, Massacussetts.

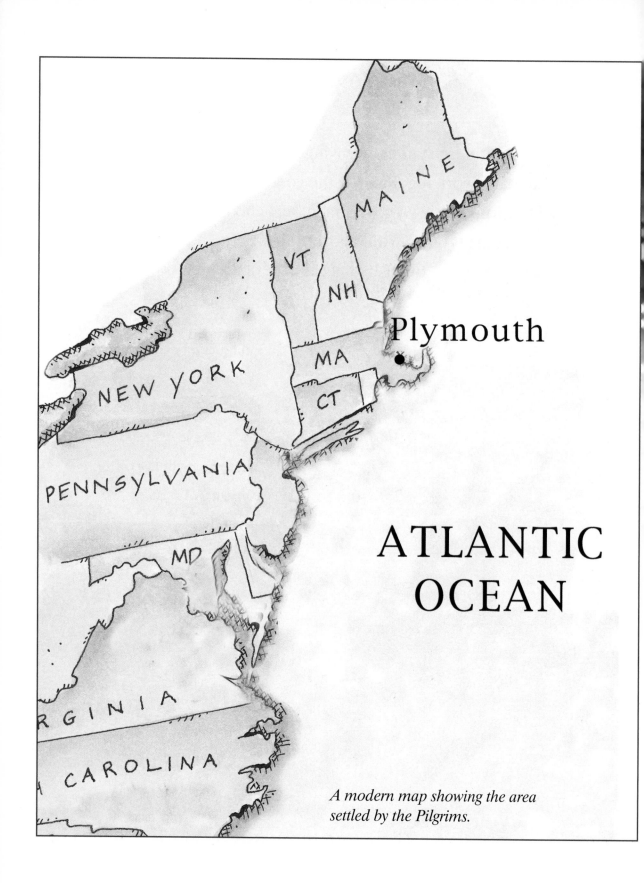

MAINE

VT

NH

MA

CT

Plymouth

NEW YORK

PENNSYLVANIA

MD

ATLANTIC
OCEAN

RGINIA

CAROLINA

A modern map showing the area
settled by the Pilgrims.

The Mayflower Compact was signed before the Pilgrims went ashore.

An agreement to work together and help one another was written and signed on November 11, 1620 (November 21, New Style calendar). That agreement is the Mayflower Compact. Among the signers were John Carver, the first governor of Plymouth, William Brewster, and William Bradford, the second governor.

Why did the Pilgrims need the compact before leaving the ship? Couldn't they have gotten to dry land first? After all, they had just completed a long and uncomfortable journey. Knowing what the Pilgrims' lives were like before their journey makes it easier to understand the necessity of the Mayflower Compact.

The Pilgrims used the Julian, or Old Style, calendar introduced by Julius Caesar in 46 BC. The Julian calendar was replaced by the Gregorian calendar, which explains why the signing of the Mayflower Compact is sometimes stated as November 21 rather than November 11.

BEFORE THE PILGRIMS

The Pilgrims' story began early in the 16th century, when King Henry VIII ruled England. Henry VIII was married to Catherine of Aragon. He wanted the Pope, the leader of the Catholic Church (and all the Christians in Europe), to dissolve his marriage to Catherine. Henry VIII claimed he wanted to end his marriage because Catherine had not produced a son to follow him as king. That was true. However, Henry wanted to marry another woman, Anne Boleyn. The Pope refused to grant the king's request for a divorce, which angered Henry VIII.

After a long and frustrating time, Henry VIII realized the only way he could get his divorce was to break away from the Catholic Church and start his own church—the Church of England. Henry VIII became the head of the Church of England, appointed people he wanted in top positions in the church, and eventually got his divorce.

When the government runs a church it is called a State Church.

William and his wife Mary worshipped at a church in nearby Babworth. Richard Clyfton was the pastor at Babworth. Clyfton was a minister of the Church of England, but he had his own views on how to deliver the word of God. Clyfton preached his religious views. He was a Separatist. Separatists all around Scrooby were meeting in secret. William Brewster opened up his home for Clyfton and his followers. Some of the *Mayflower* Pilgrims came from this group of Separatists.

William Brewster managed an inn and tavern similar to this one.

WILLIAM BRADFORD

William Bradford was just a boy when he met William Brewster. Bradford was from Austerfield, another farming town near Scrooby. Bradford lived with two uncles. Young William had an illness that made him weak, so he couldn't help with farming. Instead, William learned to read and write—a privilege for many at that time. William read the Bible and attended church.

One day William Bradford had the opportunity to attend the Separatist Church in Scrooby. Bradford met William Brewster, and they grew close. He respected and agreed with Brewster's religious views. Clyfton, Bradford, and the other Separatists continued to meet at Brewster's home until 1607.

A statue of William Bradford in Plymouth, Massachusetts

In the fall of 1607, government officials were closely watching the Separatist Church in Scrooby. It was a dangerous time for anyone who did not conform to the Church of England. King James declared "In my kingdom I will have one doctrine, one discipline, one religion, and I will make you conform or I will harry you out of this land, or worse."

The proper country name is The Netherlands. However, many called the land Holland. Holland means woodland, which describes two coastal regions in The Netherlands.

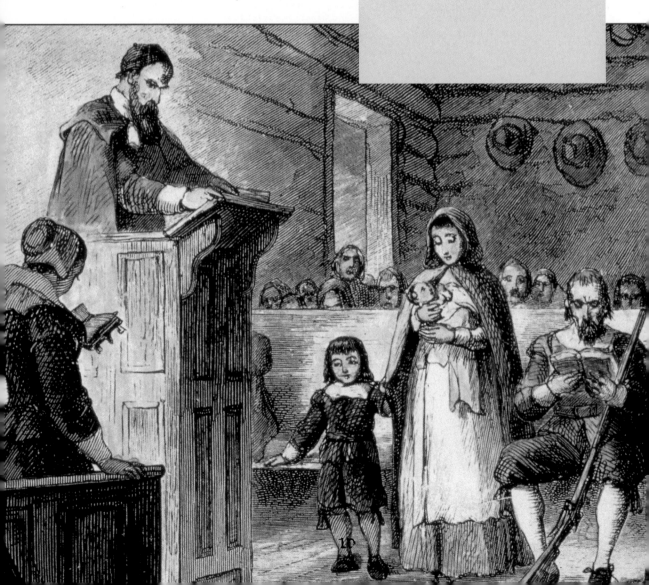

The Separatists of Scrooby, including young William Bradford, decided it was time to leave England or risk spending their lives in jail, or worse! The Separatists had no choice but to sell their homes, belongings, and land, and seek a safer existence elsewhere. They chose Holland. At the time, Holland was a place where you could practice religion freely, and other Separatist groups had fled there.

King James threatened to throw the Separatists in jail.

English Separatists worshipped despite the constant danger they were in from government officials.

ESCAPE

At the age of 17, William Bradford and the Scrooby Separatists secretly contracted a ship to take them to Holland. The group walked 60 miles (96 km) to Boston, a town on the North Sea coast of England. They carried with them possessions they wanted to take on their escape. They had arranged a secret meeting with the ship's **skipper**.

The skipper arrived late, with officers. The skipper had betrayed the Separatists. The Separatists were robbed of their money and belongings and put in jail. The Separatists posed very little threat to the king, so most of them were released, including Bradford. Brewster and Clyfton were held in prison for a month before they were freed.

The Scrooby Separatists attempted their escape again the following spring. They realized it was easier to go unnoticed if they left England in smaller groups. Eventually, they made it to Holland.

The Scrooby Separatists finally succeeded in sailing to Holland.

LIFE IN HOLLAND

William Bradford lived with the Brewster family in Amsterdam. Their Separatist group practiced their religion quietly, for a while. But, after a few months, different Separatist groups began to argue their views openly in the small community. The citizens of Amsterdam were shocked at their behavior.

The Scrooby Separatists, fearing they would lose the peaceful existence they struggled for, decided it was time to move on. Pastor Clyfton stayed in Amsterdam, but arranged for his assistant, Pastor Robinson, to find a place for the **congregation**. They moved to Leiden. It was a beautiful city on the Rhine River built on islands linked by more than 100 bridges. The people there were weavers, bakers, carpenters, and masons. The Separatists had to learn these trades in order to make a living.

The Separatists worked hard to earn a living.

In 1611, Bradford turned 21 years old and inherited his family's property in England. He sold the property and used the money to purchase a church meeting house in Leiden. The following year he became a citizen of Leiden. He purchased a **loom** and continued to practice his trade as a weaver. The next year he married Dorothy May, the daughter of another Separatist family.

By 1617, the Scrooby Separatists had been in Leiden eight years. Many of them had married and had children. Life was better, but not in all ways. The Separatists were poor. The children were growing up learning Dutch, not English. The Separatists worried about their future. They feared that Holland might soon lose its religious freedom, and everything they had fought for could be lost. Again, it was time to move on.

Dutch describes the people of The Netherlands and the language they spoke.

A loom is used to weave cloth.

CHOOSING AMERICA

The Separatists considered many places, but in the end they decided to make Virginia their new home. Virginia was the English claim of land in America.

The Separatists began negotiations with the London Company in 1617. The London Company had been granted a **charter** by King James. The charter gave the Company permission to colonize Virginia. King James finally granted the Separatists a **patent** for a tract of Virginia land in 1619, but the Separatists still needed money for their voyage.

Thomas Weston, a London **merchant**, heard about the Separatists' plans. Weston and a group of "merchant adventurers" offered to finance the trip, and the Separatists could pay them back later.

Jamestown, Virginia, was the first permanent English settlement in North America.

MERCHANT ADVENTURERS

The Separatists would have to work the land for seven years to pay back the merchant adventurers. William Bradford was a lead **negotiator** in this deal, which took months. It was June, way past planting time, and final arrangements had not been made. Weston's merchants finally chartered a vessel to sail the Separatists to America. Meanwhile, the Separatists sold their land and belongings and bought the *Speedwell* to serve as a fishing vessel in the New World.

William and Dorothy Bradford had a four-year old son, John, who did not sail with them to America. Dorothy died shortly after landing, and John would finally make it to Plymouth in 1627.

On July 22, 1620, the Separatists left Holland on the *Speedwell*. They were on their way to England to meet up with the *Mayflower*, the ship the merchants had hired.

Separatists preparing to leave The Netherlands

SAINTS AND STRANGERS

The *Speedwell*, with the Separatists aboard, docked in Southampton, England, and joined the *Mayflower* and the merchant adventurers.

The Separatists met with a group that Thomas Weston chose to take to America. They were needed to help make up the shortage of passengers required to make the voyage. These people had many skills that would benefit the new colony. Many of them were weavers, tanners, or shopkeepers. They were not Saints, as the Separatists often called themselves, so the Separatists called them Strangers.

The Separatists referred to themselves as Saints because they devoted their lives to serving God.

The Speedwell *is loaded with supplies in preparation for a long voyage.*

A LEAKY MESS

The day finally arrived when the *Speedwell* and the *Mayflower* set out to sea. After a few days at sea, the *Speedwell* turned out to be a leaky mess. The ships returned and docked at Dartmouth. It would seem that luck would never be on the Separatists' side, but they continued to have faith and hope that God would lead them to the New World.

Repairs to the *Speedwell* took two weeks. The Separatists were extremely worried now. By this time crops should be close to harvest, and they had not even planted a thing!

After the repairs, the ships set sail again. Three weeks out, the *Speedwell* was leaking again. The Separatists returned to Plymouth, England, where they decided to leave the *Speedwell* behind. The *Speedwell* passengers would all have to move onto the *Mayflower*, and there was not enough room. Some people decided to abandon their dream of freedom in America in order to make room for others. Only three members of the Scrooby Separatist congregation were on the *Mayflower* passenger list—William and Mary Brewster and William Bradford.

William Bradford leading the Separatists

THE *MAYFLOWER*

Prior to its famous voyage to America, the *Mayflower* had sailed as a cargo vessel. It carried English goods such as cloth, furs, and pewter to ports in France and Spain.

On return trips the *Mayflower* was loaded with French wine, salt, and vinegar. It was a sturdy merchant ship that made many trips before its **transatlantic** voyage.

The exact dimensions of the ship are not known, but many

merchant ships of that period were roughly 100 feet (30.5 meters) long and 25 feet (7.6 m) wide. Its decks and holds were used for cargo and supplies, and there was room for a small crew. But the ship was certainly not built to carry passengers and their belongings.

Even though the Strangers did not practice religion faithfully, together the Saints and Strangers became known as Pilgrims - people who journey on behalf of their devotion.

This replica of the Mayflower *is docked at Plymouth, Massachusetts.*

LIFE AT SEA

On September 6 (September 16, New Style calendar), 1620, The *Mayflower* took wind into its sails and its passengers left behind the English coastline for the last time. There were 102 passengers, made up of 35 Separatists and 67 Strangers. Master Christopher Jones led a crew of about 30 men.

The voyage began with warm winds and calm seas, but once at sea the conditions got worse. The *Mayflower* encountered rough seas and fierce winds. The passengers got seasick from being tossed about and were bruised from being slammed against the timbers. They wore the same clothes for the entire voyage, and most of the time they were wet.

A skipper of a naval ship held the rank of captain, while a skipper of a merchant ship was called a master.

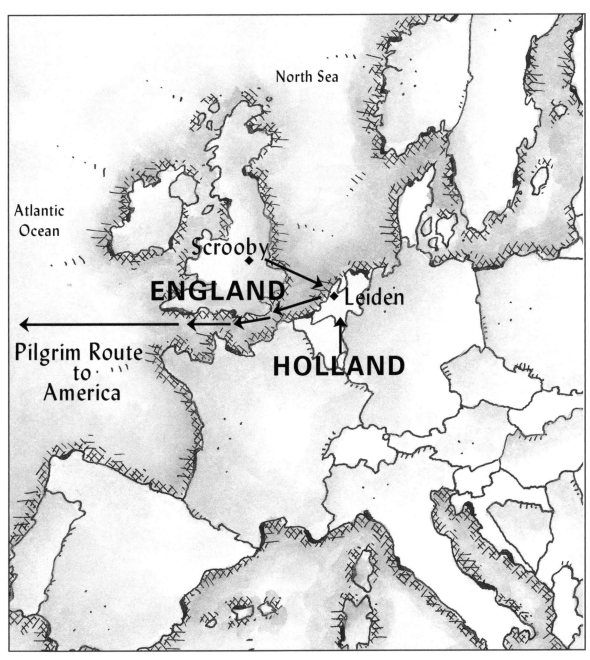

A modern map showing the Pilgrims' route to America.

Life aboard the small ship was uncomfortable in calm seas, but in stormy seas it became nearly unbearable.

The Pilgrims had very little room on board. Their living space was between decks. This was a level between the main deck on top and the cargo holds below. The ceiling was low, and the adults had to bend over to walk around.

The Pilgrims ate biscuits, salted fish, dried fruits and meats, and moldy cheese. They used spices to help cover up the taste of rotting food. A bucket in a corner served as a toilet, which was emptied overboard once a day.

The *Mayflower* became a smelly and uncomfortable ship. The Saints disliked the crew's bad language, but they prayed for them. The crew thought the Saints prayed too much and grew tired of their constant seasickness.

Only one passenger died on the voyage. However, the number of passengers stayed the same. One couple gave birth to a son, and they named him Oceanus.

LAND!

After a long, dangerous sea voyage the *Mayflower* finally reached the New World. The Pilgrims saw the shoreline of Cape Cod. It was land, but it was not the land for which they

had a patent to settle. They all agreed to sail south in search of the Hudson River, but the rough waters made it too dangerous, and the crew turned the *Mayflower* north. They anchored at the tip of Cape Cod in an area that would later be named Provincetown Harbor.

All those aboard were happy to be at their final destination, but by this time there was a great deal of tension between the Saints, the Strangers, and the crew. The crew wanted to get rid of the passengers right away. They wanted to begin their return trip before the last of their supplies were used. The Strangers argued that since they had not landed in Virginia, their patent was not legal and that no one had the right to govern the colony.

The Separatists prayed one last time on board the Mayflower *before they went ashore at Plymouth.*

THE MAYFLOWER COMPACT

William Bradford remembered some advice from Pastor Robinson; they should form a single unity with the Strangers.

A document was drawn up. All the men on the *Mayflower* gathered in the cabin of John Carver and it was read aloud.

The men aboard the Mayflower *signed the Mayflower Compact as an agreement to work together for the benefit of all.*

IN THE name of God, Amen.

We whose names are underwritten, the loyal subjects of our dread sovereign Lord, King James, by the grace of God, of Great Britain, France and Ireland king, defender of the faith, etc., having undertaken, for the glory of God, and advancement of the Christian faith, and honor of our king and country, a voyage to plant the first colony in the Northern parts of Virginia, do by these presents solemnly and mutually in the presence of God, and one of another, covenant and combine ourselves together into a civil body politic, for our better ordering and preservation and furtherance of the ends aforesaid; and by virtue hereof to enact, constitute, and frame such just and equal laws, ordinances, acts, constitutions, and offices, from time to time, as shall be thought most meet and convenient for the general good of the colony, unto which we promise all due submission and obedience.

In witness whereof we have hereunder subscribed our names at Cape-Cod the 11 of November, in the year of the reign of our sovereign lord, King James, of England, France, and Ireland the eighteenth, and of Scotland the fifty-fourth. Anno Domine 1620.

A NEW SETTLEMENT

After signing the compact, the men chose John Carver as the governor of their colony. It was the beginning of democracy in the New World.

Over the next few weeks the men went ashore to explore the area, looking for the best place to build the colony. The women and children went ashore, too. The women did laundry, and the children played and ran along the beach.

The Pilgrims began building their new settlement in December of 1620.

The Pilgrims exploring the area around Plymouth

A month after landing in Cape Cod, the pilgrims discovered Plymouth, the site Captain John Smith had named in 1614. On Christmas Day the colony began when men laid out 19 lots for cottages.

The Mayflower Compact served as the first constitution for the Plymouth Colony. The original document does not exist, but we know of it from William Bradford's journal *Of Plimoth Plantation.* The journal is at the State Library at the State House in Boston, Massachusetts.

The National Monument to the Forefathers, in Plymouth, was dedicated in 1889. It is a solid granite monument that stands 81 feet (24.7 m) tall. A tablet at the base of the monument lists the names of the Mayflower's passengers.
Plymouth Rock is on display at Pilgrim Memorial State Park in Massachusetts.

TIME LINE

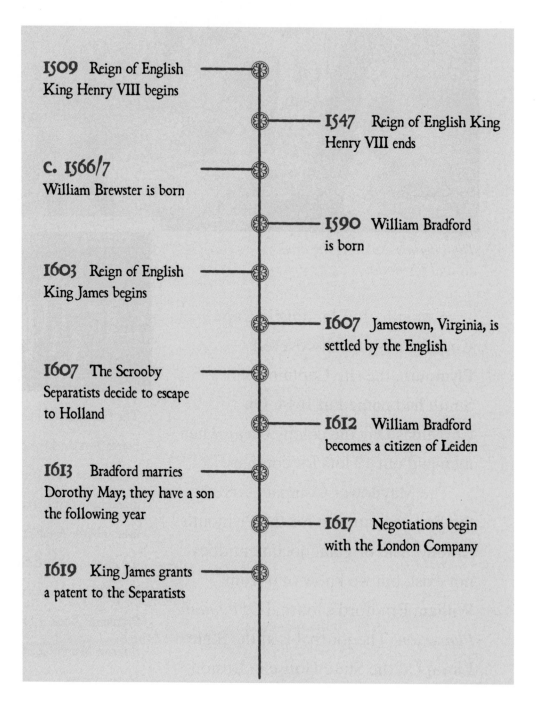

1509 Reign of English King Henry VIII begins

1547 Reign of English King Henry VIII ends

c. 1566/7 William Brewster is born

1590 William Bradford is born

1603 Reign of English King James begins

1607 Jamestown, Virginia, is settled by the English

1607 The Scrooby Separatists decide to escape to Holland

1612 William Bradford becomes a citizen of Leiden

1613 Bradford marries Dorothy May; they have a son the following year

1617 Negotiations begin with the London Company

1619 King James grants a patent to the Separatists

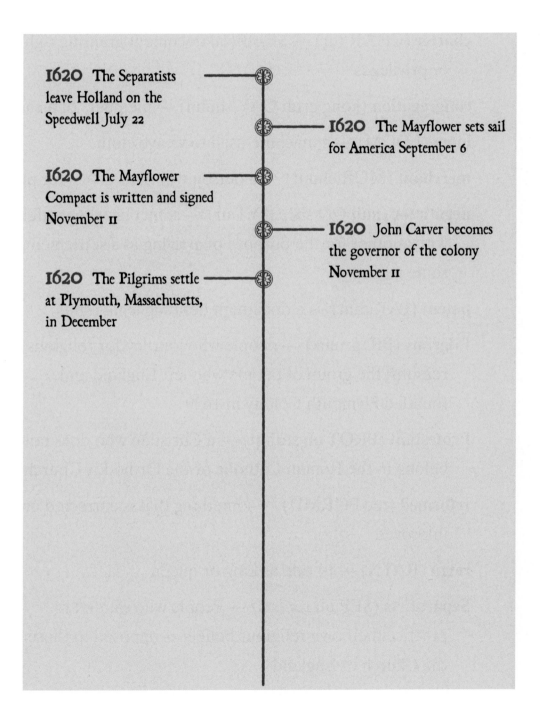

1620 The Separatists
leave Holland on the
Speedwell July 22

1620 The Mayflower sets sail
for America September 6

1620 The Mayflower
Compact is written and signed
November 11

1620 John Carver becomes
the governor of the colony
November 11

1620 The Pilgrims settle
at Plymouth, Massachusetts,
in December

GLOSSARY

charter (CHAR tur) — an official document granting rights or privileges

congregation (kong gruh GAY shuhn) — members of a church

loom (LOOM) — a machine used to weave cloth

merchant (MUR chunt) — a person who sells goods for profit

negotiator (nuh GO shee AYT ur) — someone who confers with another for the purpose of arriving at a settlement of some matter

patent (PAT uhnt) — a document defining legal rights

Pilgrims (PIL grumz) — people who journey for religious reasons; the group of people who left England and founded Plymouth Colony in 1620

Protestant (PROT uh stuhnt) — a Christian who does not belong to the Roman Catholic or the Orthodox Church

reformed (ree FORMD) — something that is corrected or improved

reign (RAYN) — to rule as king or queen

Separatists (SEP uh rut ists) — People who wanted to practice their own religious beliefs as opposed to those of the Church of England

skipper (SKIP ur) — a person in charge or in command of a merchant ship

transatlantic (tran zuht LANT ik) — crossing the Atlantic Ocean

FURTHER READING

Davis, Kenneth C. *The Pilgrims*. HarperCollins Publishers, 2002.

Schmidt, Gary D. *William Bradford: Plymouth's Faithful Pilgrim*. Eerdmans Publishing, 1999.

Whitehurst, Susan. *The Mayflower*. Rosen Publishing Group, 2002.

Whitehurst, Susan. *The Pilgrims Before The Mayflower*. Rosen Publishing Group, 2002.

WEBSITES TO VISIT

www.pilgrimhall.org/

www.plimoth.org/

www.mayflowerhistory.com/

ABOUT THE AUTHORS

David and Patricia Armentrout have written many nonfiction books for young readers. They have had several books published for primary school reading. The Armentrouts live in Cincinnati, Ohio, with their two children.

INDEX